I Am Healed
Meditating on the Scriptures

By Linda Patarello

Unless otherwise indicated, all Scripture quotations are taken from the *KJV Reference Bible*. Copyright © 2000 by Zondervan. Used by permission.

I Am Healed
ISBN: 978-0-9896919-5-6

Copyright © 2013 by Linda Patarello

Editor: Daphne Parsekian

Published by Orion Productions, LLC.
P.O. Box 51194
Colorado Springs, CO 80949
Orionproductions.tv

These small books with scriptures that fit each theme are meant to help you learn how to meditate. Each scripture has my own meditative thoughts that follow. This will help you to understand the thought flow that can happen when you think on God's Word. As you begin to think and ponder on God's Word for yourself, you will find more revelation in the Scriptures that the Holy Spirit will reveal to you personally. I encourage you to read my initial book, How to Meditate on the Living Word. That will explain in more detail the process of meditation.

This book in particular will outline what it means to be healed by Jesus. What He did for us on the cross means more than the forgiveness of sins. We will be meditating on scriptures that speak of the healing that Christ died to purchase for us.

"But his delight is in the law of the LORD; and in his law doth he meditate day and night. And he shall be like a tree planted by the rivers of water, that bringeth forth his fruit in his season; his leaf also shall not wither; and whatsoever he doeth shall prosper."

Psalm 1:2–3

"My son, attend to my words; incline thine ear unto my sayings. Let them not depart from thine eyes; keep them in the midst of thine heart. For they are life unto those that find them, and health to all their flesh."

Proverbs 4:20–22

"I beseech you therefore, brethren, by the mercies of God, that ye present your bodies a living sacrifice, holy, acceptable unto God, which is your reasonable service. And be not conformed to this world: but be ye transformed by the renewing of your mind, that ye may prove what is that good, and acceptable, and perfect, will of God."

Romans 12:1–2

It is not a waste of time to put your thoughts and your mind on God's Word—quite the opposite. You will be doing good for yourself: your body, your mind, and your future. It is rather a waste of time to worry and to only see and think on the problem. To dwell on the hopeless circumstances can only bring death.

You can choose to make a new habit. When you keep your thoughts on His Word, eventually it will come out of your mouth and you will reap the benefits from it. You will have more peace, better health, and many more positive thoughts full of life. This will happen as you give yourself to thinking on the Scriptures, but don't take my word for it—put it to the test for yourself! I would love to lead you in beginning to meditate on these things. Once you begin to understand how to meditate, you can do it for yourself. I only want to simply show you how it is done.

Many of you, I believe, will receive your healing as you allow these scriptures to come alive to you and as you imagine them real in your heart. Just as you read about these people long ago receiving their healing, you, too, will experience your own healing from Jesus of Nazareth. I'm excited for you. Let's begin…

"So Abraham prayed unto God: and God healed Abimelech, and his wife, and his maidservants; and they bare children."

Genesis 20:17

This tells us that God heard Abraham's prayers and that he heard the prayers Abraham prayed for someone else; not just someone else but his wife and their maidservants as well. God cares for all. He healed the barrenness. Servants are people too, and God cared for their well being as much as those they answered to.

"For thou hast delivered my soul from death, mine eyes from tears, and my feet from falling. I will walk before the LORD in the land of the living."

Psalm 116:8–9

If you think about this scripture in the New Testament, you could look at this verse as provision for spirit, soul, and body. Jesus has delivered your soul from death by taking your place so that you wouldn't have to die. He alone delivered your eyes from tears, for Isaiah 53:4 states, "He bore my griefs and carried my sorrows." You don't have to live in sadness. You can give it to Him and take His peace and His joy. And if you trust in Him, He will keep your feet from falling, which is speaking of your body. Through His death you have been given life. I can make the choice to take it and walk in it.

"Behold, I will bring it health and cure, and I will cure them, and will reveal unto them the abundance of peace and truth."

Jeremiah 33:6

The Lord wants to be our source for all things. He loves to care for us. It is not a chore. He does not see us as an obligation. You can suffer with symptoms of sickness for years if you want to or receive his provision by faith—receive his healing.

"Trust in the LORD with all thine heart; and lean not unto thine own understanding. In all thy ways acknowledge him, and he shall direct thy paths. Be not wise in thine own eyes: fear the LORD, and depart from evil. It shall be health to thy navel, and marrow to thy bones."

Proverbs 3:5–8

Few people trust God. Most people trust themselves, make their own plans, and decide for themselves what to do and when to do it. Can they see up ahead? No. Only God knows what's up ahead. We would do good to trust Him with all of our heart and put all of our trust in Him. Not only should we not trust ourselves, but we shouldn't even lean that way. In all of your ways, every way, acknowledge Him, think about Him and His wisdom. As you do, He shall direct your path. As you do, it will even be health to your navel and even marrow to your bones.

"Who his own self bare our sins in his own body on the tree, that we, being dead to sins, should live unto righteousness: by whose stripes ye were healed."

1 Peter 2:24

Jesus didn't have someone do it for Him. He did it Himself. He willingly bore the whole world's sin in His own body on the tree. He who never knew sin became sin for us. Sin is ugly, and sin is death. Can you imagine this? Just think of the sin of one person. Think of their whole life. Now multiply that until you have every single man, woman, and child in the whole world. There is an estimated seven billion people on this earth today. That is a heavy, heavy weight on one person. It was all put on Jesus; not only the sin but the sickness of the whole world as well. Isaiah 52:14 states that his visage (how he looked) was so marred, more than any man, and his form more than the sons of men. The next phrase says that we are dead to sins and should live unto righteousness. We died with Him, for He took our place, took our sins, and took our sicknesses and then gave us His righteousness. He paid for us to live unto righteousness. "By whose stripes ye were healed." The stripes were the lashes on the back of Jesus. He did the work on the cross. We go free from sickness and sin, but He did the work. We get the benefit.

"And great multitudes came unto him, having with them those that were lame, blind, dumb, maimed, and many others, and cast them down at Jesus' feet; and he healed them: Insomuch that the multitude wondered, when they saw the dumb to speak, the maimed to be whole, the lame to walk, and the blind to see: and they glorified the God of Israel."

Matthew 15:30–31

If we can get this picture, what an amazing picture it must have been. This doesn't say a few people, or a crowd came, but a great multitude. Once people saw miracles, they came by the droves. They were desperate. Word of mouth traveled. In many places in the gospels, it says that his fame traveled. He didn't heal and preach for fame though. He didn't have wrong motives. His motives were of pure love and compassion. Families were bringing their relatives and friends who were sick and had all kinds of different diseases. And Jesus healed them.

"And withersoever he entered, into villages, or cities, or country, they laid the sick in the streets, and besought him that they might touch if it were but the border of his garment: and as many as touched him were made whole."

Mark 6:56

He was famous! That's not what his motive was, but that's what human nature does. When someone does wonders or the unusual, the word gets around and everyone comes out of the woodwork to see. It says "withersoever," which means wherever he went. As soon as he even entered a village or a city or a country, they came; the word went out fast! He could not be alone; they followed Him everywhere! It sounds like a circus. Picture them laying the sick in the streets, making sure He would see them as He came into town. They didn't care what it looked like; they were determined to get their healing. They sought Him that they might touch even the border of His garment. As many as touched Him were made whole. It does not say they were half healed but that they were made WHOLE.

"And he arose out of the synagogue, and entered into Simon's house. And Simon's wife's mother was taken with a great fever; and they besought him for her. And he stood over her, and rebuked the fever; and it left her: and immediately she arose and ministered unto them."

Luke 4:38–39

Jesus was always teaching in the synagogue. You can picture the wisdom of God flowing out of His mouth. He arose and came into Simon's house, where his mother-in-law had a high fever. They went to get Jesus. It doesn't say that He touched her; it says He stood over her. All he had to do was rebuke the fever, which means he spoke to the fever. He always spoke with authority. It left her. She didn't just recuperate and rest for a few days. Wow, it says she got up immediately and served them! So get this picture: Not only did the high fever leave, but strength also came into her body right away. God is good!

"Now when the sun was setting, all they that had any sick with divers diseases brought them unto him; and he laid his hands on every one of them, and healed them. And devils also came out of many, crying out, and saying, Thou art Christ the Son of God. And he rebuking them suffered them not to speak: for they knew that he was Christ."

Luke 4:40–41

I love this verse and how it describes the sun setting. There are a lot of people in the world, and the strength that Jesus had to minister to so many people is astounding. "All they that had any sick" brought them unto Him. In a town or village, who knows how many this could be. But Jesus never stopped being compassionate; His mercy never ended, and so he laid hands on every one of them and healed them. This is where it was happening, which means those that were not sick were probably there to watch and see what was going on. Demons were coming out and screaming as they left, but He rebuked and commanded them not to speak. Even the demons knew who He was.

The day of Pentecost had not come yet. That's the day in the first few chapters in Acts when Jesus said to the disciples to go and wait for the power to come to them. This verse was before that day, yet they were able to cure diseases and cast out devils. They did this only because Jesus had given them power and authority to do so. And He sent them to preach the kingdom of God, two by two. They were in training; they must have been so excited. Up until then, only Jesus had done all the miracles, but now it was multiplying and growing. This is how the kingdom of God works. God the Father is all about growing, building, and blessing. He doesn't tear down people. The works of God are to build people up.

"Then he called his twelve disciples together, and gave them power and authority over all devils, and to cure diseases. And he sent them to preach the kingdom of God, and to heal the sick."

Luke 9:1–2

God gave Jesus power. And Jesus gave the disciples power—power and authority over ALL devils; power and authority to cure diseases. He sent them to preach but not to preach the law—to preach the kingdom of God. God didn't send Jesus to condemn but to save, to heal, and to show mercy. There was enough judgment already in the world. Mercy was needed, and mercy had come just in time.

He sent them to heal the sick. What an exciting day that must have been for them. They also had to overcome any fear or intimidation. A new day had dawned.

"Now when he came nigh to the gate of the city, behold, there was a dead man carried out, the only son of his mother, and she was a widow: and much people of the city was with her. And when the Lord saw her, he had compassion on her, and said unto her, Weep not. And he came and touched the bier: and they that bare him stood still. And he said, Young man, I say unto thee, Arise. And he that was dead sat up, and began to speak. And he delivered him to his mother."

Luke 7:12–15

The gate of the city is the entry to or exit from a people's way of life. Through this particular gate, there came a funeral procession of a woman who had lost her husband already and had just experienced the loss of her only son. The scripture says there were "much" people with her, but that never seemed to phase Jesus. He was focused on helping and ministering to people; He was focused on destroying the works of the devil (1 John 3:8). He was near the gate and saw as they were carrying this bier of the son out of the city. He saw her, and He must have seen deep into her heart, which was full of sorrow; He had compassion on her. He got close enough to her to speak and have her hear Him say, "Weep not."

I'm sure she knew who He was; there are scriptures that speak of how His fame was spread abroad because of all the miracles that He did. I'm betting her eyes, though full of tears, were fixed on Him even as He walked and came closer and closer. What was in their minds? It says, "They that bare him stood still." I'll bet you could hear a pin drop. What was He going to do next? Jesus dared to speak to the dead son. Who would talk to a dead person? You might talk to your loved one who is passed laying in the coffin. You might say goodbye, but you surely don't expect them to talk back. Jesus did though. He said, "Young man, I say unto thee, arise." They must have been riveted. The boy sat up and talked. I wish I could have been there to see their faces, to see her face. She must have screamed and cried for joy! Jesus delivered him to her. She had her only son back again—alive!

"And a certain man was there, which had an infirmity thirty and eight years. When Jesus saw him lie, and knew that he had been now a long time in that case, he saith unto him, Wilt thou be made whole? The impotent man answered him, Sir, I have no man, when the water is troubled, to put me into the pool: but while I am coming, another steppeth down before me. Jesus saith unto him,

Rise, take up thy bed, and walk.' And immediately
the man was made whole, and took up his bed, and
walked…"

John 5:5–9

To have an infirmity for thirty-eight years is a
lifetime. It's the same as someone being in prison for
forty years—it becomes all you know. It shapes the
picture of how you see yourself. Proverbs 23:7 says, "As
he thinketh in his heart, so is he." You have this picture
ingrained in your mind of how you see yourself, and
you have looked at it so long, you believe it is how you
are. But Jesus dared to ask the man by the pool, "Will
you be made whole?" It was a question, and He was
waiting for the man to give the answer. Instead, the
man gave an excuse. He blamed his problem on others.
But Jesus didn't let it go. He put the responsibility on
him—in fact, it was a challenge or even a command.
"Rise, take up thy bed, and walk." This was his day.
The scripture says, "Immediately the man was made
whole, and took up his bed, and walked." We must see
our healing in our mind. We must make some steps to
action. He is the healer, but we choose to be healed and
put some action to it every day.

"He healeth the broken in heart, and bindeth up their
wounds."

Psalm 147:3

He heals our body, but He is also a master at
healing our heart. He can heal every part of us because
He made us. He is our creator. He can heal our broken
heart. He binds up our wounds; the Hebrew meaning is
to wrap firmly. "Wounds" refers to sorrow or pain. Allow

Him to bandage your pain. Come to Him and receive healing for your heart, for the past. Don't live in the past any longer. Give it to Jesus.

"But unto you that fear my name shall the Sun of righteousness arise with healing in his wings; and ye shall go forth, and grow up as calves of the stall."

Malachi 4:2

To fear His name is to revere and honor Him; to have a holy fear of God, for He is awesome and powerful. To fear Him is to believe Him, and to believe in Him is to believe in His son.

One would think that the "Sun of righteousness" is a misprint, but I don't believe so. Could it be that what was trying to be said is that Jesus is so bright in His glory that He is as the sun? Righteousness comes from Him, and we are righteous in Him. He has risen in power and glory, and He has risen with healing in His wings. Healing that would fly to us; this is such a beautiful word picture—just see and imagine it. He touches us, and we receive what He has paid for. It causes us to be strong and go forth.

"And when Jesus departed thence, two blind men followed him, crying, and saying, Thou son of David, have mercy on us. And when he was come into the house, the blind men came to him: and Jesus saith unto them, Believe ye that I am able to do this? They said unto him, Yea, Lord. Then touched he their eyes, saying, According to your faith be it unto you. And their eyes were opened. ."

Matthew 9:27–30

15

It had to have taken quite an effort for two blind men to stumble and follow Jesus as He left. They were determined and didn't care if anyone saw them or heard them. They cried out. They only knew that Jesus had something they needed. They didn't think of what was proper when they cried out, "Thou son of David, have mercy on us." It says they came to Him, and Jesus said to them, "Believe ye that I am able to do this?" They said yes. He put His hand on their eyes, "According to your faith, be it unto you," and their eyes were opened. This phrase, "according to your faith," is speaking about your expectation. What were they expecting? If one of them would have said, "Well, if you could just make my body stronger so I can get around better even though I am blind," that may have been all he received, according to his faith. The Lord will meet you where you are.

"And great multitudes followed him; and he healed them there."

Matthew 19:2

This is surely a word picture. It doesn't say a few people or even a multitude, but it says a great multitude. A multitude can be a throng or a company of people, and this was a great one. Because of all the miracles, healings, and deliverances that Jesus did, word had spread quickly. He was famous whether He wanted to be or not. This is how the human nature can be; they follow the latest news and such whether it's correct or not. This doesn't mean it's the right thing to do; it's just how most people are. Some who are famous love it. Others hate crowds following them, but Jesus was always compassionate because He loved them. He was there to heal them.

"How God anointed Jesus of Nazareth with the Holy Ghost and with power: who went about doing good, and healing all that were oppressed of the devil; for God was with him."

Acts 10:38

God the Father is the one who anointed Jesus; He anointed Him with the Holy Ghost and with power. All the works that Jesus did came from the Father. He was sent by the Father, and He spoke what the Father spoke. This means that whatever Jesus did, whatever we read that He did, He did because of the Father. He told His disciples that, if you've seen me, you've seen the Father. We get a good picture of what the Father is like by looking at Jesus. Jesus went around doing good. The Father is good. Jesus didn't strike people with disease. God doesn't strike people with disease.

"And it came to pass, when he was in a certain city, behold a man full of leprosy: who seeing Jesus fell on his face, and besought him, saying, Lord if thou wilt, thou canst make me clean. And he put forth his hand, and touched him, saying, I will: be thou clean. And immediately the leprosy departed from him."

Luke 5:12–13

Lepers were usually off to themselves in a separate place because they were unclean, but this one must have heard of Jesus and came close to where He was. The Bible says that He was full of leprosy, which means He took a great risk in coming close to Jesus of being yelled at and rejected by others. He saw Jesus and fell right on his face. "Lord, if thou wilt, thou canst make me clean." He was hopeless without Jesus; there was no

17

answer but isolation, loneliness, and then death. "Thou can make me clean." He was considered dirty, and Jesus had the nerve to put out His hand and touch him. He had no fear. "I will. Be thou clean." I would love to have seen that picture in real life, but I can see it in my mind. Immediately the leprosy departed from him, and I'm sure this created no small stir.

"Jesus Christ the same yesterday, and to day, and for ever."

Hebrews 13:8

Jesus is the great I AM. The great I AM always was, always is, and always will be. This means if He is the same, so is His love and so is His power and His mercy. He always wants to heal. He always is full of power. He will never change, and His power will never end.

"My son, forget not my law; but let thine heart keep my commandments; For length of days, and long life, and peace, shall they add to thee."

Proverbs 3:1–2

Romans 5:1 says, "Therefore being justified by faith, we have peace with God through our Lord Jesus Christ." In the Old Testament, they followed the Law and the Ten Commandments. But Jesus came to fulfill the Law because we could not. Now the new commandment is to love. John 13:34 says, "A new commandment I give unto you, That ye love one another; as I have loved you, that ye also love one another." In the Old Testament, if you remembered and kept the Law, it would mean long life, length of days, and peace. Now, in the New Testament, as we love and renew our minds on His word, keeping His word in our hearts and making it first place in our lives, we see length of days, long life, and peace. These will be added to us. This is a promise we can receive in our lives.

"And Jesus went about all Galilee, teaching in their synagogues, and preaching the gospel of the kingdom, and healing all manner of sickness and all manner of disease among the people. And his fame went throughout Syria: and they brought unto him all sick people that were taken with divers diseases and torments, and those which were possessed with devils, and those which were lunatick, and those that had the palsy; and he healed them."

Matthew 4:23–24

Jesus wasn't afraid of anything or anyone, anywhere. He went all about Galilee, teaching right in the Jewish synagogues. He preached the gospel and was not intimidated at all. The gospel was the good news, and He not only preached it, but He did it. He healed all manner of sickness and disease. His fame continued to spread. People continued to bring the sick and tormented to Him, the possessed and the lunatic, the palsy; He healed them. This was His purpose. However, no matter what good He had done, people came against him. But His mercy triumphed over judgment, as seen in James 2:13.

"My son, attend to my words; incline thine ear unto my sayings. Let them not depart from thine eyes; keep them in the midst of thine heart. For they are life unto those that find them, and health to all their flesh."

Proverbs 4:20–23

This gives us a more defined way of how to meditate. You are His child; this is His instruction to you for success and health. Attend to His words. Bend your ear to hear His sayings. You come and bend your ear; you make the effort. You have to go after it. You are to let them not leave your eyes. You are either looking at the world or looking at God's Word. Keep them in the midst of your heart. They are life unto those that find them. Go and look after it; it will be life to you. His word is full of life, and his words are health to all your flesh, to every bit of your flesh, inside and out.

"For this purpose the Son of God was manifested, that he might destroy the works of the devil."

1 John 3:8

This was His purpose. His showing and life on earth had a purpose: not to judge or to condemn; not to strike you out but to strike out Satan, to destroy and annihilate the evil works of the enemy. God hates evil, not the sinner; He loves the sinner, but He hates sickness that kills, destruction that hurts, sorrow and pain that break your heart. God is for you, not against you. Get it straight; Satan hates and destroys. Satan is bad; God is good.

"And they bring a blind man unto him, and besought him to touch him. And he took the blind man by the hand, and led him out of the town; and when he had spit on his eyes, and put his hands upon him, he asked him if he saw ought. And he looked up, and said, I see men as trees, walking. After that he put his hands again upon his eyes, and made him look up: and he was restored, and saw every man clearly."

Mark 8:22–25

God will ask us to do different things sometimes to receive our healing because each person is unique. It is our obedience that is important. The blind man let him spit on His eyes. The blind man let Him put His hand upon him and lead him out of town. They must have had a bit of a walk in order to go out of town. Did they talk, and what did they talk about? Could Jesus have asked him questions? It doesn't say if they talked, but after He laid hands on him, He asked if he could see. He saw the shapes of men like trees. It's okay to lay your hands on someone again as you are praying. You are speaking to their body. You are commanding their body to obey and respond to the Word of God. He laid His hands again, and the blind man was restored and saw every man clearly. Only God could do this in a matter of minutes.

"Insomuch that they brought forth the sick into the streets, and laid them on beds and couches, that at the least the shadow of Peter passing by might overshadow some of them. There came also a multitude out of the cities round about unto Jerusalem, bringing sick folks, and them which were vexed with unclean spirits: and they were healed every one."

Acts 5:15–16

Can you picture this? It must have looked like a parade. It is amazing to think that even the shadow of the apostle Peter brought healing. Jesus is the one that provided the healing then and now. And if the Spirit of God dwells inside a person, that power is in there to bring healing to yourself and to others. That is the same power that raised Christ from the dead. Picture Peter walking by all those sick folk and those vexed with unclean spirits. They were all healed. Close your eyes and dare to picture yourself in the same spot as Peter.

You are aware of God's presence and power inside of you. You are willing to lay hands on the sick, and when you touch them, they are healed. You are the vessel, and it is His power. As you allow Him to use you and believe it, wonderful things can take place.

"I call heaven and earth to record this day against you, that I have set before you life and death, blessing and cursing: therefore choose life, that both thou and thy seed may live:"

Deuteronomy 30:19

God created life. He is all about life and blessing. God is about growing and building. Here He gives you a question, but He also gives you the answer. He doesn't want you to miss it. "Choose Life!"—that both you and your children may live. We have a choice! Choose life.

"There was a man whose right hand was withered. And the scribes and Pharisees watched him, whether he would heal on the sabbath day; that they might find an accusation against him. But he knew their thoughts, and said to the man which had the withered hand, Rise up, and stand forth in the midst. And he arose and stood forth. Then said Jesus unto them, I will ask you one thing; Is it lawful on the sabbath days to do good, or to do evil? to save life, or to destroy it? And looking round about upon them all, he said unto the man, Stretch forth thy hand. And he did so: and his hand was restored whole as the other."

Luke 6:6–10

Jesus went about doing good and healing people. So if this man was in His presence, it would have been like a magnet to the eyes of Jesus. He spotted sickness and disease from far away. He could sense it. There are guard dogs that the police use to smell drugs and such, and they are trained for this job. Jesus came to destroy the works of the enemy, so He was focused to see it. The scribes and Pharisees watched Him. They knew He would do something; they were after Him. But He was ahead of them already; He knew what they were planning. God loves to show off by doing merciful acts. Jesus saw the man, and He saw the scribes. His love was so bold. He said to the man, "Rise up, and stand forth in the midst." He asked him to stand up and stand right in the middle of the crowd, front and center; He did not want the critical scribes and Pharisees to miss one detail of this show, this act of God. He asked them the questions. Then Jesus looked all around, making sure that He had their eyes on this man. He said, "Stretch forth thy hand." His hand was restored whole as the other right in front of everyone. Praises be to God Almighty!

"And the people with one accord gave heed unto those things which Philip spake, hearing and seeing the miracles which he did. For unclean spirits, crying with loud voice, came out of many that were possessed with them: and many taken with palsies, and that were lame, were healed."

Acts 8:6–7

People gave heed because Philip spoke with authority. He had the Spirit of God. He knew who he was in Christ. People heard of the miracles God did through him, and they saw him move in miracles. Jesus told His disciples that they would do even greater works, for he was going to the Father. This goes for us as well. If the disciples did it, we can do it. Picture yourself in the place of Philip, being bold, taking your authority in Christ. Picture yourself healing those that are lame and casting out demons. They are not afraid of you alone but of Christ in you. And when you know your authority in Christ, they will cry with a loud voice and be afraid.

"Then went he down, and dipped himself seven times in Jordan, according to the saying of the man of God: and his flesh came again like unto the flesh of a little child, and he was clean."

2 Kings 5:14

The things that God asks us to do in order to receive our healing can be so different and unique to each individual. It's because He knows the heart of each individual. He loves us and wants us healed even more than we do. Thank God that He isn't a robot and that He doesn't treat us like robots, having us do the same prayer for every person. This man dipped himself seven times in the Jordan; he did exactly what the man of God said. He was obedient, and God blesses obedience. Can you imagine his flesh turning into like that of a baby? How old was this man? When you read this chapter, this man had leprosy. His skin was damaged and diseased and being eaten away. With each dip into the water, could his healing have been taking place? Could people see it? Either way he ended up with brand new flesh like a little baby. His end result was that he was clean.

"He sent his word, and healed them, and delivered them from their destructions. Oh that men would praise the LORD for his goodness, and for his wonderful works to the children of men!"

Psalm 107:20–21

He sent His word, which was Jesus. This is past tense. Each one of these verbs is past tense: sent, healed, and delivered from their destructions. Think about how many things can fit under destructions—accidents, bad habits, drug abuse, child abuse. Jesus paid the price for it all. He took the destruction on the cross. He paid for your sicknesses and for your destructions because He is a good God. And these are all part of His wonderful works. Praise Him!

"And he said unto them, Go ye into all the world, and preach the gospel to every creature. He that believeth and is baptized shall be saved; but he that believeth not shall be damned. And these signs shall follow them that believe; In my name shall they cast out devils; they shall speak with new tongues; They shall take up serpents; and if they drink any deadly thing, it shall not hurt them; they shall lay hands on the sick, and they shall recover."

Mark 16:15–18

Jesus was telling the disciples this information. He was about to go to heaven, and these were some of his last words. His charge to them was, "Go." He didn't say stay. He told them to go into all the world and preach the gospel to everyone. Everyone needs to hear the gospel. He told them that these signs would follow them that believe. Each one of these signs is supernatural, and in order to move in them, the person must believe in Jesus. If you are saved, you are eligible to move in this.

"The thief cometh not, but for to steal, and to kill, and to destroy: I am come that they might have life, and that they might have it more abundantly."

John 10:10

25

A thief does not come unless there might be something good to steal. He knows that Jesus brought life, but he doesn't want you to find it. If he can keep you away from the Word of God, he can keep you weak and unarmed. If you are unarmed, he will move right in and bring all kinds of destruction. He is even entertained by it. He hates God and anyone that God loves. He is the root of all destruction and evil. He brings destruction and then blames it on someone else. So many people in this world are walking in bitterness today from blaming God for the many years of hurt and destruction in their past because of Satan's lies. Don't fall for it.

He will get his in the end. He will be thrown into the lake of fire to be tormented day and night forever and ever (Rev. 20:10). God the Father, who is only good, will wipe away all tears from the eyes of His children; and there shall be no more death, neither sorrow, nor crying, nor pain (Rev. 21:4).

Jesus said, "I am come that they might have life." He paid dearly for us to have it. Some will partake of it, and some won't. Some will go so far as to receive His abundant life! That would be me! And let it be you, too!

"Wherefore lift up the hands which hang down, and the feeble knees; 13 And make straight paths for your feet, lest that which is lame be turned out of the way; but let it rather be healed."

Hebrews 12:12–13

To me this says to stop feeling sorry for yourself. There is no need for that! Jesus paid the price already; He paved the way for health. Pick up your hands and praise and thank Him! See yourself the way He sees you—well and whole. Push past what you are feeling and be determined to get a picture of wholeness. Keep coming back to that picture. See yourself as strong and vibrant.

"And when he thus had spoken, he cried with a loud voice, Lazarus, come forth. And he that was dead came forth, bound hand and foot with graveclothes: and his face was bound about with a napkin. Jesus saith unto them, Loose him, and let him go."

John 11:43–44

I encourage you to go to this chapter in your Bible and read the whole story to get all the details. It is very moving to picture in its entirety. In this particular account, it says Jesus cried with a loud voice. He called the name of Lazarus. Whoever was present was definitely spellbound and shaking, to say the least. Did they doubt? Did they think He was crazy to do such a thing? I don't know. But Lazarus obeyed, even all wrapped up from head to toe as he was. Jesus told them to loose him and let him go. He wouldn't need those cloths of death anymore, for he was alive! You can bet there was screaming and crying and every other kind of emotion. God was pleased to see the works of the devil destroyed. The sisters of Lazarus were pleased to see their brother. Jesus loved them, and He also was pleased to obey His Father. Nothing is impossible with God. Life comes from the Father! Death comes from Satan.

"The tongue of the wise is health."

Proverbs 12:18

If you are wise, you will speak health and speak life. The very fact that this person is speaking health says that they are thinking health for the tongue is one of the last steps of the meditation process. Your words are the fruit of what is in your heart. First the imagination, then the thoughts are built, then the seeds are planted in your heart. A root is built, and the tree grows. Finally the fruit comes out of the mouth, and then the action takes place. If you are wise to begin with, you will dwell on thoughts of healing, not fear and sickness.

"Pleasant words are as an honeycomb, sweet to the soul, and healthy to the bones."

Proverbs 16:24

Speak words of life. Don't speak doom and gloom. Think words of thankfulness and gratefulness. Count your blessings. Think on the good things like the scripture in Philippians 4:8: "Whatsoever things are of good report; if there be any virtue, and if there be any praise, think on these things." Think of the times that people spoke words that were cruel to you. You don't forget those times. You can go way back to when you were a child, and you have those memories. These can have an effect on you and even your body. So if that's so, it can go the opposite way as well. This verse says that pleasant words are healthy to your bones. That means that the words of our mouth are that important! They affect the very bones of your body, your very core.

"And, behold, a woman, which was diseased with an issue of blood twelve years, came behind him, and touched the hem of his garment: For she said within herself, If I may but touch his garment, I shall be whole.

But Jesus turned him about, and when he saw her, he said, Daughter, be of good comfort; thy faith hath made thee whole. And the woman was made whole from that hour."

Matthew 9:20–22

When a woman had any problem with an issue of blood, she was considered unclean and needed to be separate from people, somewhat like the lepers stayed to themselves. But this woman was desperate and took the risk of being found out. She had to have thought out a plan. She must have even pictured how it could all possibly work out. For it says, "She said within herself, if I may but touch his garment, I shall be whole."

Maybe she figured since she was unclean, she wouldn't be able to speak to Him, but if she could sneak through the crowd and just touch Him that would be enough. She was expecting it. She came, and she did as she had planned. Jesus turned around and felt the power leave Him. He saw her, and maybe she was frightened that she was caught, but He had too much compassion to be angry. "Daughter, be of good comfort; thy faith has made you whole." Others would have shouted obscenities at her; she was used to that. But Jesus was gentle. And she was made completely whole from that hour.

"Bless the LORD, O my soul, and forget not all his benefits: Who forgiveth all thine iniquities; who healeth all thy diseases; who redeemeth thy life from destruction."

Psalm 103:2–4

We have no need for weeping. We have no need for complaining and whining. We should stir our own self up and say, "Hey, get with the program, Soul! Start counting your blessings! Start looking at all the good God has done in your life. It all adds up. Start counting what Jesus has paid for you and me." Even if you have experienced much tragedy and pain in your life, you can still thank Him for all the spiritual blessings. If you know Jesus, you have eternal life. And when you get to heaven, you have a mansion waiting in glory and a strong, healthy young body. You can have that even now in this life, but you must learn how to receive by faith, how to speak to your body. Learn to see yourself as God does.

"A merry heart doeth good like a medicine; but a broken spirit drieth the bones."

Proverbs 17:22

How do we get a merry heart? It starts with the imagination and planting those seeds into your mind, which then begins to root down in your heart. It can't help but erupt out of your mouth when it does. You have to choose to get your mind off of your problems and think on the Word of God. We must realize that the Word of God is positive. It wasn't until I began to meditate on His Word that I began to realize that. I used to think it was boring. I was so wrong. Another way to get yourself happy is to worship! Turn on the worship music and start dancing, even if you don't feel like it. It will get you going, and before you know it, you will really feel it.

"But if the Spirit of him that raised up Jesus from the dead dwell in you, he that raised up Christ from the dead shall also quicken your mortal bodies by his Spirit that dwelleth in you."

Romans 8:11

This is amazing to imagine—the Spirit that actually raised Jesus from the dead lives in you. He stays in you. He never leaves. Where you go, He goes. And He loves you like He loves Jesus. As He quickened Him, this verse states He will ALSO QUICKEN your mortal body. This means to make alive. Whatever is going on in your body, this verse says He can bring life. You can speak life every day. "The Lord is bringing life to my body as He brought life to Jesus."

"To be carnally minded is death; but to be spiritually minded is life and peace."

Romans 8:6

Think on good things. Keep your mind on things above. Think about Jesus and seeking to get closer to Him and to know Him, for this is our goal. These things bring life and peace. When we are focused on things like unforgiveness, strife, gossip, self pity, complaining, the lust of the flesh, and such, this all will be sure to bring death—a sure slow death.

"He giveth power to the faint; and to them that have no might he increaseth strength. Even the youths shall faint and be weary, and the young men shall utterly fall: But they that wait upon the LORD shall renew their strength; they shall mount up with wings as eagles; they shall run, and not be weary; and they shall walk, and not faint."

Isaiah 40:29–31

He gives power to the faint. It comes from Him. When we are weary, we have somewhere to go to be strengthened and refreshed. If you have no might, He will increase your strength. He is able, and if the Word says, 'He will do it,' then that means He is also willing. It's up to us just to come. Any person on Earth lives in a human body. This means, at some point, we get tired. Even the young get tired, and they are full of youthful energy. But, they that wait upon The Lord, no matter what age, will renew their strength. The wingspan of an eagle can be up to 8 feet long. They are strong, and The Word often compares the believer to them. The eagle flies high and courageous, never fearing a storm. They know how to handle it. You shall run and not be weary. You shall walk, and not faint.

"Surely he hath borne our griefs, and carried our sorrows: yet we did esteem him stricken, smitten of God, and afflicted. But he was wounded for our transgressions, he was bruised for our iniquities: the chastisement of our peace was upon him; and with his stripes we are healed."

Isaiah 53:4–5

Surely. This begins with surely. As they watched, they thought God was punishing Him. Because He had declared He was God, He was being rightfully punished and tortured. They were ignorant of what was really going on. It is done. Healing rightfully was paid for us.

"And being not weak in faith, he considered not his own body now dead, when he was about an hundred years old, neither yet the deadness of Sarah's womb: He staggered not at the promise of God through unbelief; but was strong in faith, giving glory to God; And being fully persuaded that, what he had promised, he was able also to perform."

Romans 4:19–21

This is speaking of the journey of Abraham and his faith. How could he be strong in faith even though he had not seen the promise fulfilled? God had promised them a son, but he was old and Sarah was old and barren. He didn't deny the circumstances that were there, but he chose to not consider them. He chose to focus, instead, on the promise of God. He magnified that promise, and he gave glory to God. This is where he stayed. The more he did this, the stronger his faith became until one day he was fully persuaded. You see, you can get to the point where you believe God, and you know that you know that you know you've got it. Inside you have this clear picture. And no one can take it from you. Then, it's just a matter of time before you will see it.

"Now the just shall live by faith:"

Hebrews 10:38

If you are in Christ, you are considered just; you are the righteous ones in Jesus. This is how you should live: by faith—not by what you feel, or what you see, but by faith. We should live by trusting God and taking Him at His Word. He is faithful and true. His Word will never pass away. Isaiah 54:10 says, "For the mountains shall depart, and the hills be removed; but my kindness shall not depart from thee, neither shall the covenant of my peace be removed, saith the LORD that hath mercy on thee."

You please God when you live by faith because that's how He lives. When you live this way, you are saying, "I believe that Jesus paid the full price on the cross for me."

"Beloved, I wish above all things that thou mayest prosper and be in health, even as thy soul prospereth."

3 John 1:2

He is speaking to believers. If you will read the last part first, that is the key. Your soul must prosper first. What does this mean? The way for a soul to prosper is first to believe in the Son of God and then to be filled with the knowledge of His Word, so much so that it is planted in your heart, growing deep roots. As Psalm 1 says, when you meditate on his Word day and night, the end result will be that you will prosper in all that you do. So as your soul prospers, the rest of your life will also. It begins from the inside out. See a healthy body. See a life that has blossomed in every way.

About the Author

Linda Patarello is a born again Christian, and graduate from Charis Bible College in Colorado Springs, Colorado. She currently lives there, and spends most of her time spreading the truth about God's Love from the written Word. Linda is a California native with broad experience in leading praise & worship and songwriting. She believes that the highest calling is to worship the "Giver of All Gifts." She also believes we are born to pursue a relationship with God the Father, Jesus Christ and the Holy Spirit, and to share it with others. Her vision is to help people find true love for the Word of God, and to uncover its precious truths that are waiting to be revealed.

For More Information or to Contact the Author, Please Write to:

Linda Patarello
P.O. Box 7964
Colorado Springs, CO 80933

www.Heartsower.com

Prayer of Salvation

There is nothing more fulfilling in life than knowing that God loves you. God has made, and continues to make His love known to us by having sent His only begotten son, Jesus Christ, to die on the cross as payment for our sins and the injustices done unto us.

Has anyone willingly given up their life in exchange for yours, so that you may live? Jesus did. "Greater love hath no man than this, that a man lay down his life for his friends" (Jn. 15:13). Notice, that Jesus said this *before* he went to the cross. He laid down His life for us because he saw you and I, his friends, benefiting from this act of love.

You were the joy that was set before Jesus. "For the joy that was set before him [he] endured the cross, despising the shame, and is set down at the right hand of the throne of God" (Heb. 12:2). Only a true, selfless friend could love like this. Would you like to know the One Who finds you valuable, Who truly loves you? If you would like to ask Jesus to be your friend and your Lord and Savior, you can ask Him today. You can use your own words or pray,

"Lord Jesus, I want to know you, I want to be your friend. I invite you into my life, so that I may know you more. Be my saving friend, Lord and Savior. I am sorry for all my sins and past mistakes. Thank you for forgiving me and loving me, in spite of my past. You are my friend, even when I have no one else. I want to receive everything you have for me, even your Holy Spirit. Take control of my life, and through my relationship with you, let it grow and mature, and become a light unto others. Thank you for freeing me from sin and darkness, and for putting me in right-standing with you forever. I am saved! Thank you, Jesus! Amen!

If you prayed this prayer for the first time in your life, we believe that you are born again! Find a good Bible-based church, and connect with other believers. Please share your testimony or visit us online:

http://www.orionproductions.tv/contact-us.html

You can write to us:

Orion Productions

PO Box 51194
Colorado Springs, CO 80949

Blessings to you! From our staff at Orion Productions.

*To make known the stories and accounts
of God's work in people's lives
through multimedia products and
services.*

*Our latest publishing information can be found
by visiting our website at:*

www.orionproductions.tv/publishing.html